D1214479

Baseball and Softball

GETTING THE EDGE: CONDITIONING, INJURIES, AND LEGAL & ILLICIT DRUGS

Baseball and Softball

by Gabriel Sanna

Mason Crest Publishers

MASON CREST PUBLISHERS INC.
370 Reed Road
Broomall, Pennsylvania 19008
(866)MCP-BOOK (toll free)
www.masoncrest.com

First Printing
9 8 7 6 5 4 3 2 1

Library of Congress Cataloging-in-Publication Data

Sanna, Gabriel.
  Baseball and softball / by Gabriel Sanna. — 1st ed.
      p. cm.
  Includes bibliographical references and index.
  ISBN 978-1-4222-1730-6   ISBN (set) 978-1-4222-1728-3
  1. Baseball—Juvenile literature. 2. Softball—Juvenile literature. I. Title.
  GV867.5.S265 2010
  796.357—dc22
                              2010007227

Produced by Harding House Publishing Service, Inc.
www.hardinghousepages.com
Interior Design by MK Bassett-Harvey.
Cover Design by Torque Advertising + Design.
Printed in the USA by Bang Printing.

The creators of this book have made every effort to provide accurate information, but it should not be used as a substitute for the help and services of trained professionals.

Contents

Introduction

GETTING THE EDGE: CONDITIONING, INJURIES, AND LEGAL & ILLICIT DRUGS is a four-teen-volume series written for young people who are interested in learning about various sports and how to participate in them safely. Each volume examines the history of the sport and the rules of play; it also acts as a guide for prevention and treatment of injuries, and includes instruction on stretching, warming up, and strength training, all of which can help play-ers avoid the most common musculoskeletal injuries. Each volume also includes tips on healthy nutrition for athletes, as well as information on the risks of using performance-enhancing drugs or other illegal substances. GETTING THE EDGE offers ways for readers to healthily and legally improve their performance and gain more enjoyment from playing sports. Young athletes will find these volumes informative and helpful in their pursuit of excellence.

Sports medicine professionals assigned to a sport with which they are not familiar can also benefit from this series. For example, a football ath-letic trainer may need to provide medical care for a local gymnastics meet. Although the emergency medical principles and action plan would remain the same, the athletic trainer could provide better care for the gymnasts after reading a simple overview of the principles of gymnastics in GETTING THE EDGE.

Although these books offer an overview, they are not intended to be comprehensive in the recognition and management of sports injuries. They should not replace the professional advice of a trainer, doctor, or nutrition-ist. The text helps the reader appreciate and gain awareness of the sport's history, standard training techniques, common injuries, dietary guidelines, and the dangers of using drugs to gain an advantage. Reference material and directed readings are provided for those who want to delve further into these subjects.

Written in a direct and easily accessible style, GETTING THE EDGE is an enjoyable series that will help young people learn about sports and sports medicine.

—*Susan Saliba, Ph.D., National Athletic Trainers' Association Education Council*

1
Overview of Baseball

Understanding the Words

Amateur *is someone who plays a sport only for fun, not to make a living.*

Regulation play *consists of the first nine innings in most baseball games. (In a Little League game, however, regulation play is only six innings long.)*

Scouts *are people who look for talented players to add to their teams (either college or professional).*

The History of Baseball

If someone mentions "America's favorite pastime" or "our national game," you know the subject is baseball. True, football is equally popular, and basketball is the only world-famous sport invented in the United States, but because it was our first popular game, baseball has a special place in the nation's heart.

Baseball's season begins in the springtime and lingers through the warm summer months and on into the fall. Americans created it from an English school game called rounders, which has been played since the 1700s. One English alphabet book published in 1744 even listed it under "B" for "base ball." Rounders is more like softball, however, using a softer ball that is pitched underhand. Only two "bases" were originally used, marked by poles instead of bags. Players were out if the opposing team threw the ball and hit them as they were running to first base or between bases, so only a soft ball would do.

Some early American versions of baseball had different names, such as "old cat," "goal ball," "town ball," and the "Massachussetts game." One of the main developers of the U.S. game was Abner Doubleday, who laid out a baseball field in 1839 in Cooperstown, New York, and played one of the first official games. (Appropriately, the National Baseball Hall of Fame is now located in Cooperstown. And Doubleday, who has even been given credit for "inventing" baseball, later became a Union general during the Civil War and was a hero at the Battle of Gettysburg.)

A number of individuals in New York in 1845, including Alexander Cartwright, a surveyor, drew up the first set of rules for our modern-day game. Throwing the ball at the runner was outlawed for the first time. Amateur New York teams such as the Knickerbockers, Gothams, and Empires used these rules for their 1846 season. Soldiers playing in camps during the Civil War spread this version around the country.

Professional teams appeared when the war ended in 1865, and the National Association of Baseball Players was established in 1870. Its teams

Baseball has been played professionally for more than a century in the United States. The first World Series was held in 1903.

included two familiar names: the White Stockings of Chicago and the Athletics of Philadelphia. Many of these teams did not survive, however, such as the Kekiongas of Fort Wayne, Indiana; the Forest Citys of Cleveland, Ohio; the Mutuals of New York; and the Eckfords of Brooklyn. The association

"Babe" Ruth (1845-1948)

George Herman "Babe" Ruth has been called "the most domi-
nant player in history." His record of sixty home runs in one
season (1927) was not broken until 1961, when seasons themselves had become longer; and his career record of 714 home
runs lasted until 1974, when Hank Aaron hit his 715th home
run.

Ruth began as a pitcher for the Boston Red Sox, pitching
twenty-nine and two-thirds scoreless World Series innings
for them. But the Babe was such a
powerful hitter that he was shifted
to the outfield, meaning that he
could bat in every game. The New
York Yankees bought him in 1920
for $125,000 (today worth almost
$1.5 million), which proved a wise
investment. His fourteen seasons
of home runs earned him the title
"Sultan of Swat," and Yankee Stadium is still called "the house that
Ruth built."

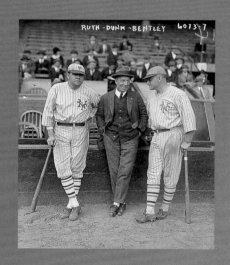

During his career, Ruth scored 2,174 runs and batted in 2,211
more. His slugging average of .847 in 1920 remained the
record until Barry Bonds beat it in 2001, with .863. He was so
dangerous at the plate that pitchers walked him 2,056 times.
Ruth retired in 1935, at the age of 40.

broke up in 1876 when the National League of Professional Base Ball Clubs formed. The American Association began as a rival in 1891 and later became the American League. The two "major leagues" were now in place, and the World Series began in 1903.

The Basic Rules of Baseball

A team has nine players, and each game lasts nine innings. The visiting team bats first in the "top half" of each inning, and then plays defense while the home team bats in the "bottom half." If tied after regulation play, the game continues until one side is ahead after any extra inning.

Baseball is played on a field called a "diamond." Each diamond has three bases (sometimes called bags), a home plate where the batter stands, and a mound on which the pitcher stands.

Jackie Robinson (1919-1972)

Major league baseball had no African-American players until 1947, the year Jackie Robinson joined the Brooklyn Dodgers at second base. It was a good move because Robinson was named Rookie of the Year, and two years later he became the National League's Most Valuable Player. He played on six pennant-winning teams in his ten years with Brooklyn, including the 1955 World Series championship team.

Born in Cairo, Georgia, Robinson played four sports at UCLA before signing in 1946 with Brooklyn and being assigned to the Dodgers' farm team in Montreal, Canada, where he led the league in batting. Moving up to Brooklyn the next year, he proved an excellent hitter, achieving a career batting average of .311. He was also a daring base runner, leading the league twice in stealing bases and stealing home nineteen times.

After he retired in 1956, Robinson turned to politics, particularly the Civil Rights Movement. In 1962, he became the first African American named to the Baseball Hall of Fame.

Play ball!

Jackie Robinson was the first African-American player in major league baseball when he joined the Brooklyn Dodgers in 1947. In 1962, he was the first African-American baseball player to be inducted into the Baseball Hall of Fame.

Play ball!

The bases, or bags, are at the corners of a square that makes up the infield "diamond," and there is a distance of 90 feet (27.4 meters) between each base. The pitcher stands in the center on the "mound," which is elevated 10 inches (25 centimeters) and delivers pitches to each batter at home plate, which is 60.5 feet (18.4 meters) from the mound. The ball itself has a circumference of about 9 inches (23 centimeters) and the bat a maximum length of 42 inches (107 centimeters). A batter tries to hit the ball far enough—hopefully into the outfield—to advance to one or more bases. If four pitches are thrown outside the batter's strike zone, the batter receives a free "walk" to first base. A batter hit by a pitch can also go to first base.

The pitcher's mound is 60.5 feet from home plate and raised ten inches off the ground.

Runs are scored when a player moves around the bases, returning to home plate. A ball hit inbounds over a fence is a home run, which lets the batter make a free circuit of the bases. The batting side is retired after three outs in an inning. A player can be called out for several reasons:

- letting three good pitches go by, either by swinging and missing or by not swinging, known as a strikeout.

- hitting a ball that is thrown to first base before the player can run there, or throwing him out.

- hitting a ball that is caught in the air by a defensive player, known as a fly out.

- running between bases and being touched with the ball by a defensive player, which is called a tag out.

- having to advance to the next base because another runner is behind and a defensive player touches the base first, also called a force-out.

The defensive infield players are the pitcher, catcher, first baseman, second baseman, shortstop (between second and third bases), and third baseman. The three outfield players are the left fielder, center fielder, and right fielder.

The History of Softball

You might say that softball is baseball's little brother. It has more players than any other U.S. team sport, with more than forty million people playing the game during the summer months. Like baseball, it is an exciting game of skill, but its smaller playing field makes it even faster.

Softball also has other advantages: boys, girls, men, and women of any age can play, the equipment and uniforms are relatively inexpensive, and amateur leagues can be quickly formed by schools, churches, and businesses. It is an ideal informal game at picnics and other outings.

The Amateur Softball Association, which is the national governing body of the sport in the United States, has more than 250,000 official member teams with four million players. This includes its youth program of more than 80,000 teams, which has some 1.3 million players ranging from under ten years old up to eighteen.

The game was invented in 1887 on a cold winter day in Chicago, when George Hancock saw someone in the Farragut Boat Club toss an old boxing glove at another person who hit it right back with a stick. Hancock chalked off a small baseball field in the club's gym, and two teams of friends played the first game of "indoor baseball," finishing with a score of 41–40. The next

Softball was invented in 1887. In the United States, more people play softball than any other team sport.

spring, Hancock organized games around Chicago on fields too small for baseball, changed the name to "indoor-outdoor," and drew up nineteen rules that were adopted in 1889 by the Mid Winter Indoor Baseball League of Chicago.

People quickly realized the advantage of a sport that could be played in small public parks and on school playgrounds. Other cities took up the game, especially Minneapolis, where fireman Lewis Rober used a small medicine ball for the games he organized on a vacant lot to keep firemen in good condition during their off hours. His team was nicknamed the Kittens, and the local game became know as "kitten ball" until 1925, when the Minneapolis Park Board renamed it "diamond ball." Other areas called the game "mush ball" and "playground ball." The next year, however, Walter

The official rules of softball weren't in place until 1923.

Play ball!

Mark McGwire (1963-)

"I can't believe I did that," said the St. Louis Cardinal's Mark McGwire on September 27, 1998. "It blows my mind. I am almost speechless. I've amazed myself." In fact, he amazed everyone, for McGwire had just hit his seventieth home run of the season in his last game, breaking the seasonal record set thirty-seven years earlier by Roger Maris of the New York Yankees.

"Big Mac," who stands six feet, five inches (1.95 meters) and weighs 250 pounds (113 kilograms) had joined the Oakland Athletics in 1986, becoming the American League Rookie of the Year and helping the Athletics to with the 1989 World Series. Oakland would regret trading the first baseman to St. Louis in 1997, when he blasted fifty-eight home runs, a year before the record seventy.

McGwire, however, began to have injury troubles. In 2000, he missed games because of a back injury, and the next year went zero for twenty-nine at bats while recovering from knee surgery. Still, big McGwire has assured his superstar status. As the cardinal manager, Tony La Russa, said of McGwire's abilities after his seventieth home run: "He's stranger than fiction."

Hakanson, a Denver YMCA official, suggested "softball." By then, the game was well established in Illinois, Minnesota, Wisconsin, Colorado, and Florida.

SOFTBALL GOES OFFICIAL

In 1923, the National Recreation Congress in Springfield, Illinois, began to draw up new official rules of play. The nonprofit Amateur Softball Association (ASA) was founded in 1933 in Newark, New Jersey. That same year, it adopted the rules, then quickly organized a tournament that was held at the Chicago World's Fair. Based since 1966 in Oklahoma City, Oklahoma, ASA now has more than eighty levels of play for youth and adult men and women, including teams for men over seventy-five years old. In 1973, it dedicated a National Softball Hall of Fame, which by 2003 had inducted 126 members, including players, managers, umpires, and administrators. The organization also has a Softball Museum and Hall of Fame Stadium for national tournaments.

Like baseball, the amateur game of softball has spread around the world. It was even an Olympic sport in 2000, when the U.S. softball team won the gold medal in Sydney, Australia. The International Softball Federation (ISF) in Plant City, Florida, has member organizations in 124 nations; even China has a Softball Association. The ISF collects and sends used equipment valued at $200,000 a year to overseas teams and holds world championships for men and women. It also has an overseas International Softball Federation Hall of Fame, which by 2003 had ninety-two members from twenty countries.

THE RULES OF SOFTBALL

Although similar to baseball, softball has important differences. First, the game is shorter, having only seven innings. Second, the field is smaller, as is the bat, which is a maximum of 34 inches (86 centimeters), which is 8 inches (20 centimeters) shorter than the bat used for baseball. Also, the ball is larger, with a circumference of about 12 inches (30 centimeters), or some 3 inches

(7.5 centimeters) larger than a baseball. The ball is pitched from a flat area, not a mound. Two types of softball games have also developed, the fast-pitch and the slow-pitch versions.

Fast-pitch softball, with nine players, is closer to baseball. However, the ball is pitched underhand, the strike zone extends from the armpits to the knees, and runners can leave their bases only if a pitch has left the pitcher's hand. The distance between bases is 60 feet (18.2 meters), and 40 feet (12.2 meters) for women. Teams are usually single-sex.

Soft-pitch softball has ten players, the extra "rover" player being in the outfield. The ball must be pitched higher, 6–12 feet (1.8–3.6 meters) above the ground. The strike zone is from the top of the shoulders to the knees. A batter who fouls off the third strike is out. Stealing bases is not allowed, and a player is out who leaves a base before a pitch reaches the plate or is hit. The distance between bases is 65 feet (19.8 meters), and from the pitching plate to home plate is 46 feet (14 meters) for both men and women.

Opportunities to Play Baseball

Playing baseball offers a great advantage to anyone wishing to become a professional athlete. The sport offers training and competition from the age of five, and a player can then advance through layers of increasingly difficult competition.

ELEMENTARY SCHOOL BASEBALL

It is easy for a child to join a baseball or softball league. The Little League, founded in 1938, has some three million participants in baseball and softball in nearly one hundred countries. The League offers T-ball for children ages five to eight. Its older divisions for both baseball and softball are Little League, for those ages nine to twelve, Junior League, for ages thirteen to fourteen, Senior League, for fourteen- to sixteen-year-olds, and Big League, for those

DID YOU KNOW?

Former President George W. Bush was once a Little League player.

who are sixteen to eighteen. Its Challenger League is for mentally and physically challenged players from five to eighteen years old.

The Babe Ruth League, established in 1951, has nearly one million participants in its baseball and softball programs in the United States and Canada. It runs a Cal Ripken baseball league, for kids who are five to twelve, and older divisions for teenagers who are thirteen to fifteen and sixteen to eighteen. The softball divisions are for those twelve and under, sixteen and under, and eighteen and under.

Among the other excellent youth training grounds are the Dizzy Dean and Dixie Youth leagues.

Kids and teens are able to play baseball and softball in leagues created specifically for them. Little League is a baseball league for kids ages 9-12, for example.

Joe DiMaggio (1914-1999)

Joe DiMaggio became known worldwide in 1954 for marrying Marilyn Monroe, but his real fame in American was as the "Yankee Clipper" outfielder who helped New York win ten pennants and nine World Series. The son of Italian immigrants, he joined the Yankees in 1936 and was known for his class both on and off the field.

DiMaggio was named the American League's Most Valuable Player (MVP) three times. He led the league in homers in 1937 with forty-six and again in 1948 with thirty-nine, after serving in the army during World War II. His career had many highlights, but the most remarkable was his streak of hitting safely in fifty-six consecutive games in 1941, a record that still stands. His batting average that year was .406.

Almost as remarkable was DiMaggio's ability to play with a series of injuries. When DiMaggio retired at the age of thirty-seven, he said, "I was full of aches and pains." He was named to the Baseball Hall of Fame in 1955.

Joe Di Maggio led the New York Yankees to nine World Series victories. He was named Most Valuable Player (MVP) three times by the American League.

Play ball!

JOE DI MAGGIO
Salutes His Bat

© 1941..The Sporting News Pub. Co.

HIGH SCHOOL BASEBALL PROGRAMS

Many high schools have fine baseball and softball programs. This is the place to make your mark and catch the attention of college and even professional **scouts**. More than 455,000 students play high school baseball, but only six out of every one hundred seniors will advance to play men's baseball on a team for a college or university of the National Collegiate Athletic Association (NCAA).

One way to increase the chance of playing ball with your favorite college is to attend its summer baseball camp. A week's instruction may cost several hundred dollars, but this is an opportunity to meet a school's coaches, who look upon the camp as a good recruiting tool. Colleges sign many players who attend their camps.

SCHOLARSHIPS

Colleges and universities offer baseball scholarships to the best high school players. The largest schools are in the NCAA's Division I, and they are allowed an average of 11.7 full scholarships, while the Division II programs have nine full scholarships. Some schools in both divisions do not fully fund all available scholarships. There are none offered by Division III colleges. Member schools of the National Association of Intercollegiate Athletics (NAIA) each have twelve full scholarships, and the schools in the top two divisions of the National Junior College Athletic Association (NJCAA) are allowed twenty-four available full scholarships. Other programs exist, such as the Professional Baseball College Scholarship Plan, sometimes offered by Major League clubs as part of a player's contract. The Babe Ruth League also has a College Scholarship Program for players who participated in its baseball and softball divisions.

Colleges and pro scouts and even sports agents will be drawn to high school players who have the potential to be drafted by major league clubs.

Many leagues exist for teens to play baseball in organized settings, improving their skills and enjoying friendly competition.

Most players, however, need to work very hard to attract a college scholarship bid. Remember that failing academic grades will quickly end the dream. If you are a student doing well in the classroom in your junior year, send out contact letters to college coaches and also ask your high school coach to recommend you to the preferred program. By your senior year, you could phone the college to ask for a tryout on campus. Even if you end up making the team without the benefit of a scholarship, intercollegiate baseball is a showcase for talent and is one step closer to the professional game.

Play ball!

Cal Ripken Jr. (1960-)

Cal Ripken Jr. is one of the most famous baseball players in the world—but he didn't get that way because of his statistical achievements. What Ripken is known for is this: his refusal to take a day off. He holds the world record for most games played in a row—2,632.

Ripken started out playing high school ball—and went straight from there to Baltimore Orioles in 1978 at the age of seventeen. He played his entire twenty-one-year career with Baltimore.

On the evening of September 6, 1995, Ripken played his 2,131 consecutive game, breaking Lou Gehrig's 56-year-old record. Once the record became official in the fifth inning, fans at Baltimore's Camden Yards gave Ripken a twenty-two-minute standing ovation. Ripken's long "Streak" helped Americans fall in love all over again with baseball.

Ripken continued to play through the 2001 season, joining the 3,000 hit club in 2000. He finished his career a 19-time All-Star with 3,184 career hits, 431 career home runs, 1,695 career RBIs, and a .276 career batting average. He was nearly unanimously voted into the Hall of Fame on January 10, 2007.

Play ball!

Cal Ripken Jr. never missed a game in his career. After 2,632 games, he holds the world record for most games played in a row.

Through 2000, the major school that has won the most College World Series, the NCAA's baseball championships, was the University of Southern California (USC) with twelve. However, since 1990, Louisiana State University (LSU) has won the most with five. Texas and Arizona State have also won five over the years, and the University of Miami, Florida, has taken three titles.

The NCAA also holds a Women's College World Series for softball, which was won by the University of Arizona in 2001 and the University of California in 2002.

Students who play baseball or softball can sometimes get college scholarships based on their athletic performance.

PLAYING FOR THE MINOR AND MAJOR LEAGUES

In all, there are more than 25,000 baseball players attending NCAA schools, and fewer than eleven of every one hundred senior players go on to be drafted by a major league team. Remember, however, that there are thirty major league teams and that these major league teams have minor league "farm" clubs, such as the teams in the Triple-A International League and Pacific Coast League, which are used to develop players.

Making it in the big leagues has long been the dream of many American children from all over the country. President Dwight Eisenhower once recalled a summer afternoon when he was a small boy fishing on a Kansas riverbank with his friend. "I told him that I wanted to be a real major-league baseball player," said Eisenhower. "My friend said that he'd like to be the President of the United States. Neither of us got our wish."

2
Mental Preparation and Safety

Understanding the Words

Visualization *means to picture something in your mind.*

Visualization

As in all sports, positive motivation can give a player the extra strength needed for victory. If you are convinced that you are prepared and you are confident of winning, the game is almost won. We all can tell when a team is "up" for a game, being inspired to play better than normal. Perhaps their motivation comes from the fact that this is a crucial contest, or they wish to avenge a previous defeat or win for a retiring coach. Whatever the reason, the players are mentally fired up.

Baseball and softball players also use this mental conditioning to play a safer game. The technique, known as visualization, helps reduce nervousness and increase confidence. If you are a pitcher who will be facing a dangerous batter, for instance, you can visualize striking out your opponent with a clever mixture of your best pitches. You can also imagine making your best moves on the field without being reckless and inviting injuries. Rehearse

Visualizing success can often yield positive results in athletic competition.

in your mind the times that you have slid safely into home plate, handled a line drive in the infield, or leaped and thrown over a runner at second to complete a double play. Remember that you can build up a positive self-image by controlling your attitudes and emotions.

Sports psychologists say negative thinking or a bad attitude can actually cause injuries. If you control anxiety and anger, you will play better and safer.

Superstitions

The game of baseball is full of superstitions, many of which are as old as the organized game itself. Maybe following these rules really does help teams win, and maybe they do not; you decide!

- Tap your bat on home plate before you bat.
- Don't shave after a first post-season win.
- Don't wash all or part of your uniform during a winning streak.
- Mentioning a player's statistics while he is doing well will jinx him.
- Don't step on the foul line when jogging onto the field.
- Never talk about a perfect game or no-hitter in progress.
- Hold on to a lucky bat or glove.
- Don't talk about how a 7-game series will end before it is finished.
- Chew only one wad of gum per game.
- Eat the same food or go to the same restaurant before every game.

Play ball!

This is so important that professional baseball teams have sports psychologists on their staffs who work with players on mental conditioning. Most players, of course, do not have such professional help and must rely on themselves and on pep talks with other team members to learn how to relax, gain confidence, reduce stress, and avoid injuries.

Visualization, or mental imagery, is especially important and can be practiced days or hours before a game. Find a time and place to relax, then picture yourself in a game, remembering the way the stadium looks and the views and sounds that you will experience from your position on the field: the grass, the bullpen, the scoreboard, the dugout chatter, even the fans roaring their approval at your play. Imagine hitting a homer into the bleachers, stealing a base, or catching a fly ball against the outfield fence to retire the team at bat.

Injuries will also be fewer when you increase your concentration during the game. Whether batting or playing defense, you can be both "psyched up" and calm at the same time. This "relaxed attention" can be increased by talking to yourself: "Here comes the fast ball," "Watch out for the bunt," "He'll be running on the next pitch," and so on. You can also hear relaxed chatter among the infield players as they encourage each other. Good players enjoy the competition and are not too anxious and tense about their batting and fielding. They know that it is not the end of the world if they strike out or commit an error. Many more opportunities will come to a well-trained player.

Equipment

Although baseball and softball players have to stay alert to avoid injuries, the easiest way to have a safe game is to wear protective equipment. The U.S. Consumer Product Safety Commission estimates that more than 58,000

Confidence Builds Confidence:
Brett Lawrie

When Brett Lawrie was selected sixteenth overall by the Milwaukee Brewers in 2008, he was an ordinary Canadian teenager—with a lot of talent. But Brett knew that talent has to be used.

"There's obviously a lot of pride," he told the media on the back porch of his home on draft day. "It's great; it's the best feeling I've had ever. It's one of these moments in your life that you only get one time so you have to take everything in. It's been a real fun day."

Brett's pride motivated him to go on to shine at the World Junior Championship in Edmonton, where he took home three awards: the Top Hitter Award, the Most Home Runs Award (3), and the Most RBIs Award (16). He was named the catcher for the World All-Star team.

Brett's amazing summer continued when he was chosen to play on Canada's Olympic men's baseball team at the Beijing Games in August 2008. He joined his sister Danielle, a pitcher with the Canadian women's softball team, at the Games in China.

Play ball!

baseball injuries to children, or nearly 36 percent of all baseball injuries, would be prevented or reduced by wearing proper protective equipment.

Being struck by the ball is the major danger, especially in baseball. Many injuries to young players from a batted, pitched, or thrown ball are due to the player's unskilled response. The standard baseball is made of a core of cork or rubber, which is wound with fibers, such as cotton or wool, and then covered with two pieces of leather sewn together with 108 stitches. It can be pitched at

Each baseball has 108 stitches holding two pieces of leather together, covering the ball.

more than 90 miles per hour (145 kilometers per hour), so hard that helmets are required for batters in organized leagues. And when hit strongly with a high-tech aluminum bat, the ball may be propelled at far more than 100 miles per hour (160 kilometers per hour), so all defensive players must always wear gloves.

The pitcher is in special danger from a batted ball. Little League records show that in a single year, emergency room treatment was needed for twenty-eight injured baseball pitchers and ten softball pitchers, from five to eighteen years old—and the numbers are higher for older players. Fortunately, better safety programs have meant that these totals have since fallen. All players should also wear shoes with rubber spikes to reduce injuries.

THE CATCHER'S EQUIPMENT

The catcher occupies the most dangerous position on the field and wears the most protective equipment. Otherwise, he would be injured by foul balls or a wrongly swung bat. The gear is jokingly called "tools of ignorance" because it supposedly protects the catcher from his own mistakes. As well as the mitt, the catcher's protection should

Catchers are required to wear special protective gear so that they are not injured by a baseball or softball.

Play ball!

Catchers must use special mitts that are larger than the average mitt, and have protective padding that other gloves do not.

include a helmet, face mask, chest protector, throat protector, shin guards, and a protective supporter cup. All this may look like a burden, but modern equipment is lightweight and provides good freedom of movement.

During a game, the catcher will handle more than 150 pitches. The leather mitt, therefore, is vital for protecting hands and fingers. It should always be worn during practice sessions and warm-ups. The mitt has extra padding and is 15.5 inches (39 centimeters) from top to bottom, which is 3.5 inches (9 centimeters) longer than a fielder's glove. Amateur players should never use a fielder's glove if they are playing catcher.

The catcher's helmet and facemask are light but strong. A helmet usually has vinyl on the outside and leather inside. The masks have a steel framework, and some newer ones are made of a new resin compound advertised to be stronger than steel. Both versions of the mask can be flipped up. The mask is on properly when it is squarely over the face and tightened with the adjustable straps. Individual "goat's beard" throat protectors can be attached to hang from the bottom, but many masks have a built-in wire extension that is 2 inches (5 centimeters) long. Some have side deflectors built in for extra ear protection. As with the glove, helmets and masks should always be worn during a practice or warm-up, as well as for games.

Catchers wear a helmet with a facemask during games and practice alike. The mask can be flipped up, but is worn down during play.

The catcher's long-style padded chest protector covers the upper chest, abdomen, groin, collarbone, and lower neck. Shin guards should fit perfectly to protect from bruises, so catchers wear their baseball shoes when choosing guards to make sure they are the correct length. A shin guard should cover the kneecap, shinbone, and lower leg, and should also have wings to protect the ankle and foot. Most versions add an extended instep plate.

PLATE UMPIRES, BATTERS, AND FIELDERS

The plate umpire, who stands directly behind the catcher, wears similar additional protective equipment. This includes a padded body protector, now normally worn underneath the shirt, which covers the chest, shoulders, and upper arms. The umpire's mask needs to provide protection to the side of the head and the throat. It should also offer excellent visibility, enabling the umpire to make accurate decisions.

Batter's Helmet

The first protective helmets for batters were worn in 1938, and today's batters are required to wear them. The plastic shell has foam padding inside and extends to cover the ears. The helmet should fit snugly on the head without the back rim resting on the neck, and the bill should not be too low on the forehead because that would block the player's vision. Ordinary baseball caps should not be worn under helmets.

The batting helmet does not, however, protect the face. Youth baseball and softball players have more face, eye, and mouth injuries than players in any other sport. Safer versions of helmets are available and include either a wire face mask or a transparent plastic shield to cover the face from the tip of the nose to below the chin. This extra protection for the face is required by the Dixie Youth Baseball organization. Batters can also add plastic goggles, custom-fitted mouth guards, forearm and wrist guards, ankle guards, and shock absorbers worn over the second and middle fingers.

Fielders' Gloves

Fielders' gloves measure about 12 inches (30 centimeters) long and are 8 inches (20 centimeters) wide. The infielders' gloves are slightly smaller because of the quick play required, but the first baseman has a longer webbing to snag fast throws. Fielders also protect their eyes by wearing sports goggles.

Batters have worn helmets since 1938.

Baseball Bats

"The first step to hitting," said Mickey Mantle, the Yankees' famous hitter, "is to find the right bat." And there are many choices. The famous Louisville Slugger was first made in 1884, and in 2003 the company produced 1.4 million of them for professional and amateur players.

Professional teams must use wooden bats, which are shaped, sanded, and given a natural or flame-burned finish. These have traditionally been made of white ash, but recent years have seen a trend toward maple or a combination of the two. Maple bats do not break as easily and they hit further. Barry Bonds of the Giants used maple to hit his record seventy-three home runs in 2001.

Light and long-hitting aluminum bats were first used in 1971 and have been popular since the 1980s with teams in youth leagues, high schools, and colleges. If professionals switched to them, however, players would score so many home runs that the stadiums would have to be expanded.

Play ball!

Other Safety Equipment

A safety-release base may help prevent the injuries caused in organized play when younger players slide into bases; every year, more than 6,600 players are injured in this way. The safety-release base is anchored to rubber mats, and if it receives a hard knock, it will pop away, leaving no parts sticking out of the ground and no holes in the ground.

3
Physical Preparation

Understanding the Words

Ligaments *are the tough material in your body that fastens together bones with other bones.*

Aerobic *has to do with exercise that requires your heart and lungs to work hard to bring oxygen to your cells.*

Growth plates *are the parts of your bones that grow, allowing you to become taller and bigger as you get older.*

Rotational *means something that turns.*

Your **hamstring** *is the tendon at the back of your knee.*

A **tendon** *is a tough flexible band (a little like a rubber band) that fastens your muscles to your bones.*

A **regimen** *is a system for doing the same thing the same way.*

Efficiently *means to get something done in the easiest way while achieving all the result you need to have accomplished.*

Warming Up

One of the best ways to prevent baseball or softball injuries is to warm up before each game or practice, because cold muscles are more likely to be injured, and stiff muscles cause clumsy play. Increased flexibility will make it easier for you to respond more quickly in a game. Besides warming the muscles, warm-up exercises will stretch them, as well as the ligaments and other connective tissues. Such exercises are also aerobic, so your heart and breathing rates will also increase, supplying additional oxygen to your body's system. Even a warm-up of five to ten minutes will have a positive effect. This could include simple walking or running in place, followed by jumping jacks. We've all seen players warming up at their positions on the field: players making relaxed throws around the infield, pitchers tossing the ball in the bull pen, and upcoming batters swinging in the on-deck circle.

Stretching is very important, and each major muscle group needs a pre-

Upcoming batters warm up by taking practice swings in what is called the "on-deck circle."

game workout. Throwing is the movement most used in the games of baseball and softball; pitchers, catchers, infielders, and outfielders must all protect their throwing arms. To help avoid sore arms and injuries, try these stretching exercises:

- Let one arm hang loosely next to the body. Then take the elbow with your other hand and pull the arm until the biceps touch your chin. Hold for five to ten seconds. Then change arms and repeat. Do this two or three times for each arm.

- Place one arm on the back of your head, then put your other hand on the top of the elbow, and pull it lightly for five to ten seconds. Switch arms and repeat. Again, do this two or three times for each arm.

Tossing the ball back and forth is a great way for players to warm up their throwing arms.

Throwing is also the most common pregame warm-up done on the field:

Two players stand 25–40 feet (7.6–12.1 meters) apart and toss the ball back and forth about a dozen times. Use a big circle movement of the arm in order to stretch the shoulder and rotator cuff. Increase the distance to 45–65 feet (13.7–19.8 meters) for about ten throws. Players who are twelve years old or younger should not throw at this longer distance, which might cause injuries.

Pitchers can warm up with fifteen to twenty-five throws before a game, but at no longer a distance than their regular pitches during a game. It is important to

Pitchers must be careful of injuring themselves while playing. In Little League, for example, pitchers are only allowed to pitch one game per week to avoid the chance of injury.

limit the number and types of pitches thrown by a young pitcher. Serious injuries can occur to a player's **growth plates**, where bone growth occurs near the joints. Too much stress placed on the elbow and shoulder can cause damage, even a chipped bone, which would ruin the possibility of a baseball career. The Little League limits pitchers to one full game (six innings) a week. The American Sports Medicine Institute (ASMI) recommends certain numbers of pitches for young players pitching two games a week: seventy-five for ages thirteen to fourteen, seventy for ages eleven to twelve, and fifty for ages nine to ten.

Pitchers who are eleven or younger are also advised not to throw curveballs, as these involve a snapping motion of the wrist and put pressure on the arm, all of which could cause serious damage.

Baseball and softball are games that often require rotating or twisting your body in the same direction. Think of a shortstop, who constantly cuts off a ground ball and turns quickly to throw it to first, or a batter swinging at pitches, always from the same side of the plate. Repeating these moves over and over can cause **rotational** strains and pains. These can be minimized by a warm-up that includes a few light rotation moves, such as holding your hands straight out in front of you and rotating in both directions, as if swinging an imaginary bat. Then pick up the bat for easy practice swings in both directions, back and forth. This will warm the muscles on both sides and help avoid a "corkscrew" injury caused by twisting.

Other warm-up exercises could include:

• Sit, then hold each foot separately while you rotate the ankle. This will help avoid ankle sprains.

• Sit, then reach forward to grasp your ankles. This will help prevent **hamstring** pulls or sprains.

• Stand, then bend at the knees, and stand, then touch your toes. These exercises will help you avoid back and thigh injuries.

Players should also keep their muscles warm in the dugout when their team is at bat. Walking around a bat is better than sitting out a long half inning. Also, players should briskly jog back onto the field, rather than trudging back to their positions. These small efforts will help to keep players lively and alert when this is needed in the late innings. After a game, players should also do light walking and stretching to help the heart and body gradually slow down.

The Importance of Flexibility

Obviously, strength and speed are very important in the game of baseball. The modern professional game is filled with fast and explosive plays, and anyone who cannot perform these tasks instantly is sure to be left behind. Because of this, players often perform the same motion repeatedly or stay in a certain position, such as a shortstop twisting to throw to first base often, or a catcher holding his mitt in the same position throughout the game. Doing the same thing over and over like this decreases the flexibility of your muscles. If this happens, sudden or strong movements outside the usual range of motion can cause injuries such as ligament or **tendon** tears. Here are a few stretches that you should do before and after every practice and game, to keep these joints flexible and to decrease the risk of injury:

• Lie on your back, bend your knees, and let them fall to one side. Keep your arms out straight to either side of you, and let your back and hips rotate with your knees.

• Stick one arm straight out in front of you. Rotate your wrist down and outward, and then use your other hand to gently continue to rotate your hand upward.

• Stand up straight, and place your hand behind the middle of your back with your elbow pointing straight out to your side. With your other hand, reach over and gently pull your elbow forward.

Physical Conditioning

A regular physical conditioning program throughout the year (not just during baseball season) will provide additional protection against injuries, such as those caused by overusing muscles. This program can be a combination of running, swimming, cycling, and other exercises, such as push-ups, pull-ups, and sit-ups. Aerobic conditioning is needed to avoid fatigue, and strength-and-endurance training can help reduce injury and also promote health. Good strenuous physical activity for twenty to thirty minutes, three days a week, will greatly improve a player's endurance.

Young players, however, should avoid heavy strength training, including weight training, resistance training, and plyometrics. All players, no matter

Young baseball and softball players should avoid intense strength training, while maintaining physical fitness with exercises like push-ups or running.

their age, need to avoid too much training as the baseball and softball seasons approach. Training that is too long or too vigorous can lead to extra tiredness, stress, and poor performance on the field.

WEIGHT TRAINING

Weight training is a way to increase the size and strength of muscles by harnessing the force of gravity in various forms. There are two common types of equipment used to achieve this. The first are free weights or barbells, which

consist of weighted disks placed on a bar, which is lifted by the athlete. The other types of equipment used in weight training are weight machines, which use weights placed on sliders or cables, which a person must then push or pull to move. Weight machines tend to be safer than free weights because it is impossible to drop the weights on yourself, and they are specifically designed to exercise one muscle or group of mus-

Lifting free weights are a great way to add weight training to your exercise routine without needing special equipment.

cles at a time. By lifting the same amount of weight many times and gradually over time increasing the amount lifted, an athlete can strengthen her muscles.

Weight training is extremely valuable in the sport of baseball because of the many fast, strong motions that a player must make. However, it is easy to strain yourself during weight training by attempting to lift more than you can handle. When starting a new weight lifting routine, you will be exercising muscles that have likely never been used very much before. Overusing these muscles can lead to serious injury. Also, there is always the danger of dropping a weight on yourself, no matter how experienced you are. For these reasons, no new weight-lifting **regimen** should be started without consulting an expert, and you should never lift weights without someone else nearby to help you. Also, weight training has negative effects on the developing skeletons of young people. When you have not finished growing, weight training wears down the growth plates on your bones, which keeps your bones from growing fully and results in stunted growth. Therefore, if you are under seventeen, you should not begin a weight-training regimen.

RESISTANCE TRAINING

Resistance training is a form of strength training in which a person is working against some force other than gravity. An example of this is the use of elastic bands; by shortening the band, one can easily increase resistance. The benefits of resistance training are many, and include increased muscle strength and size, as well as greater bone density. Unlike weights, elastic bands do not put the same kind of stress on joints and bones, and instead help to strengthen them. Studies have shown that resistance training has decreased the frequency not only of joint injuries, but of lower back injuries and muscle strains as well.

Resistance training has many positive effects, as it helps to strengthen both joints and muscles, but athletes should still take care not to strain themselves with any new resistance training program. As with any new regimen, an expert should be consulted beforehand, and you should ease into your new program to allow your body to adapt to the new stresses and to avoid unnecessary strain.

PLYOMETRICS

Many athletes do not rely on strength training alone to help them build the speed and power they need to react quickly on the field. They also use plyometrics to build this power. Plyometrics are high-intensity exercises with many exaggerated motions. The principle behind plyometrics is that when you stretch a muscle before it has a chance to contract, it contracts with more force than usual, which improves muscle tone and strength, as well as flexibility. Some examples of plyometric exercises include:

- Jump from a small box and rebound off of the floor onto a higher box.
- Stand with one foot in front of the other. With your front knee behind the toe, bend into a lunge. Jump up and switch your legs in midair, landing in a lunge with the opposite foot in front.
- Place your feet together. Bend your knees until you are squatting, and jump as high as you can. Land in a squatting position, and repeat this for up to one minute.

While plyometrics are another important tool in building the strength and speed necessary for the intensity of baseball, using this technique without proper preparation can lead to injuries. Most of the injuries sustained during plyometrics are due to bad form. For example, landing the wrong way on your foot over and over again can gradually strain your foot until injury is inevitable. That's why you should always have an expert teach you the correct form for plyometric exercises. Attempting plyometrics without any strength training can also result in overstraining the muscles, since most plyometric exercises take advantage of gravity to put a greater load on your body than usual. As with all new exercise programs, you should ease into it slowly so that your body has a chance to adapt to the new demands being placed on it.

CARDIO TRAINING

Increasing the strength and speed of your muscles is not the only thing you need to work on to improve your baseball game. Cardiovascular training, usually just called "cardio training," helps to strengthen your heart and lungs, as well as train your body to use oxygen more efficiently. These exercises can help build your endurance so that you can play for longer without becoming tired. Some of the best cardio exercises are as simple as running and swimming, as well as biking, rowing, and cross-country skiing. All these exercises should be performed for at least thirty minutes at a time to get the full effect.

Cardio training is not without its own risks. Exercises such as running produce repeated impacts against your ankles and knees, so you should be sure to wear the proper footwear and practice the best possible form to lower the risk of injuring these areas of your body. Swimming is one cardio exercise that cushions your joints completely, with much less risk of injury than other forms of cardio activity. In addition, depending on the stroke you use and your range of motion, swimming can greatly improve your flexibility.

4
Common Injuries, Treatment, and Recovery

Understanding the Words

Inflammation *is the way your body's tissues often respond to injury with pain, swelling, redness, and heat.*

Cartilage *is the tough elastic material found between your joints and in your ears and nose.*

Physical therapy *is treatment for injuries that involves exercises and massage.*

Rehabilitation *is the process of getting something (or someone) back into normal working condition.*

An **ultrasound** *is a device that sends high-frequency sound waves into body tissue. It is used to create images of the body's internal structure, but it is also sometimes used to create heat in injured tissues.*

More injuries happen in baseball and softball than in even the high-contact sports of football, basketball, and hockey. One reason, of course, is that more people play on the diamond, facing many chances of being hit by the ball, which is the most frequent cause of serious injury and even death.

Every year nearly 500,000 injuries related to baseball are treated in emergency rooms, physicians' offices, clinics, and hospitals. This does not even include unreported "minor injuries," such as bruises, cuts, and sprains, which are treated with first aid by a coach, another player, or a parent.

As mentioned, many injuries can be prevented by a physical-conditioning program, warming up before playing, staying alert during the game, and by wearing the proper protective equipment. The fast action of the game, how-

More injuries happen in baseball and softball than in any other sport. Each year, there are around half a million injuries caused by baseball, for instance.

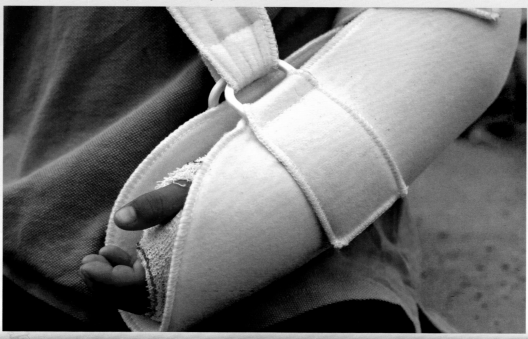

ever, ensures that injuries will happen sometimes, even from the simplest plays, such as throwing the ball or rounding a base. The most important thing is to not ignore the pain, so that you can receive immediate treatment and determine whether the injury is serious.

The most common baseball and softball injuries happen to the shoulders and arms because a player makes so many throws. Injuries also occur to the head, knees, and ankles when players collide, runners slide into bases, and fielders dive to make catches. Fractures are common, and many different bones, from fingertips to legs, are cracked, shattered, or broken.

Shoulder and Arm

Injuries to the throwing shoulder are very common. During a professional baseball season, about one-third of the players on the disabled list have shoulder injuries, and in some years these have caused a total of 6,000 missed days of play. The injury is often

Around one out of every three injured professional baseball players have a shoulder injury.

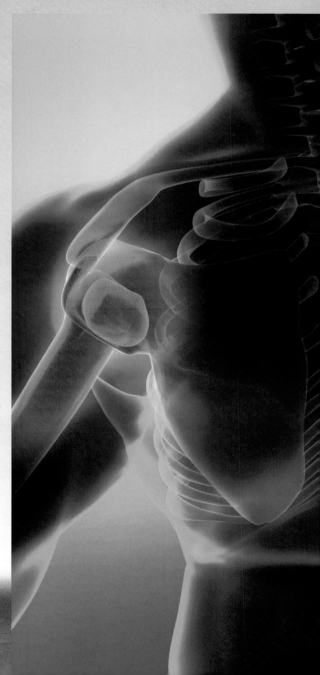

Play ball!

described as tendonitis, inflammation, or strain, and it is an overuse injury caused by throwing the ball over and over. As a result, a shoulder pain may come and go for a while, and then become progressively worse. Tendonitis means **inflammation** and pain in the tendons, those tough, fibrous tissues that connect muscles to bones. Baseball players, especially pitchers, often get rotator cuff tendonitis when the tendon tears by rubbing the under part of the shoulder. The rotator cuff is the capsule of tendons and muscles that surround the upper arm and holds the shoulder together. Injuries cause pain on the outside of the shoulder, with pain and weakness when lifting the arm.

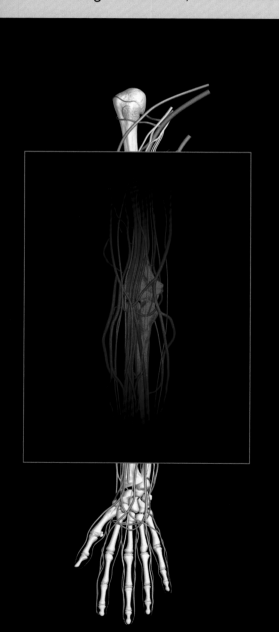

"Little League elbow" is a serious injury that can be caused by making a throwing motion repeatedly. Young players who have this injury may risk permanent damage.

Young players, who are still growing, should not ignore pain in the shoulder because the stress of throwing can damage the **cartilage** when growth occurs. A player can even fracture the growth plate in the shoulder or suffer a shoulder separation, a serious ligament tear in which the end of the collar bone, or clavicle, rises up. Any of these problems require X-rays and can be treated successfully by rest from the game, **physical therapy**, or, in the worst cases, minor surgery.

"Little League elbow" is another type of stress damage caused by constant throwing. It is important to recognize the symptoms early (symptoms include a twinge, tightening, or burning sensation in the muscle). Little League elbow occurs just the below the elbow at the inside top of the arm bone, an area of bone which is not yet completely hardened in young players. Often the cartilage is also injured, which can harm the proper movement of the joint throughout life. This is why Little League has limits on the number of throws a pitcher can make (two hundred a week or ninety in a game) and also tries to limit a pitcher throwing the curveball because this motion snaps the elbow down. An injured elbow must be X-rayed, and treatment includes the R.I.C.E. program (see sidebar). If a pitcher gets Little League elbow, she may have to rest the arm for six to eight weeks, or until the pain goes away. A pitcher may still play other positions and bat if this does not cause pain. Cartilage damage requires a longer period of rest and medication, and surgery is sometimes needed.

Head and Neck

Head and neck injuries usually come from the player being hit by the ball. The Consumer Product Safety Commission studied 88,700 injuries from being hit by a ball and found that 29.5 percent of the injuries were to the head and neck. Players can also injure these areas by colliding or sliding into a base. The most dangerous head injury is a concussion, which is an injury to the brain

R.I.C.E.

"Rest, Ice, Compression, and Elevation" —a treatment program most often applied to sprains and strains. The following steps should take place twenty-four to forty-eight hours after an injury.

- **Rest**. Do not use the injured area; this may even mean bed rest. Serious injuries, such as a broken arm, require immobilization (usually with a cast) for a short period. The time needed for rest varies, depending on the injury.
- **Ice**. Put ice on the injured area as soon as possible. This is effective in the first two or three days. Apply ice two or three times an hour for twelve to twenty minutes each time. Use an ice pack or crushed ice in a plastic bag. Never put ice directly against the skin; wrap it in a towel and keep in place with a bandage—or place a thin piece of cotton between the ice and skin.
- **Compression**. Wrap an elastic bandage snugly around the injured area, being careful not to wrap it tight enough to cut off blood flow.
- **Elevation**. Raise the injured area above your heart level, if possible. You can use pillows as props.

Play ball!

that might cause a player to lose memory, be unconscious, or, in rare cases, die. Symptoms include a severe headache, nausea, or confusion. If a batter's helmet is damaged by a throw, the force involved could also be enough to cause a concussion. A player who is unconscious should be taken quickly to the doctor. Depending on the severity of the concussion, players will have to skip play for a minimum of seventy-two hours to about one month.

Neck injuries include those in which the nerves are stretched, causing temporary numbness and a stinging pain (hence this injury's nickname, "stinger").

If treated incorrectly, or by people who are not experts, a neck injury can be very serious, or even life-threatening.

Injury Causes a Change of Plans

Aaron Richardson was dead set on making all-state baseball his senior season.

That all changed in the blink of an eye for the Byron High School senior. Aaron, a catcher, was injured on a play at the plate. He sprained his knee and was sidelined for two weeks—a serious blow to his all-state dreams.

"It was disappointing," he said. "It was a brand new experience. It was different sitting and watching rather than playing."

But Aaron didn't sulk—he made the best of the situation. His team struggled in his absence and he played the role of a coach.

"I would calm them down if they had a bad inning," he said. "I helped with whatever they needed."

Aaron finally got to return to the field on Thursday and said it felt great. He also learned a thing or two about himself during his time out. "Don't take it for granted," he said. "It's a gift you shouldn't take lightly."

His mother, Pam Richardson, said she was proud of her son during the ordeal. "He is the most positive person I ever met," she said. "He always makes the best out of a situation."

(From an article by John Foren that appeared in the *Flint Journal* on May 18, 2009.)

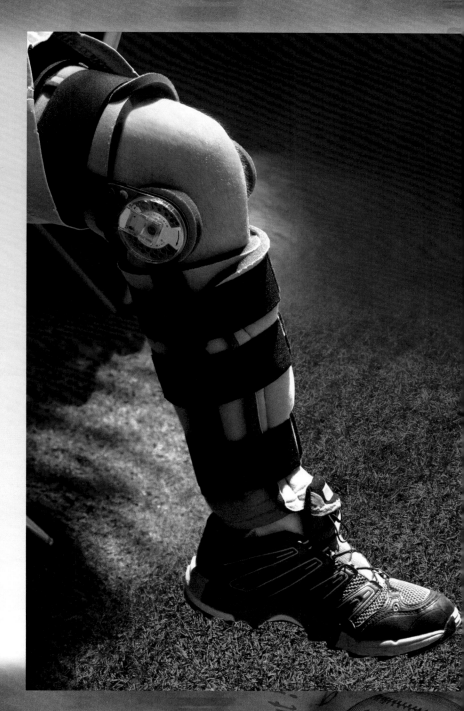

Players may need to wear a brace after a particularly serious knee or ankle injury. Minor sprains can often be treated with a combination of rest, ice, compression, and elevation (RICE).

Play ball!

This, however, is minor in comparison to a fracture or injury involving the spinal cord. Only qualified emergency personnel should move a player who is lying on the ground with a serious neck injury, because movement could cause paralysis or death. Treatment for minor injuries will require a neck collar or brace, followed by exercise to strengthen the neck.

Knee and Ankle

Knee injuries can occur during any action on the field. The knee's connecting tissues can be stretched or torn by a runner turning or sliding, a fielder twisting for a fly ball, or a pitcher making a delivery. A sprain is a partial or complete tear of a ligament, while a strain is the same injury to a muscle or tendon. You will know you have a sprained or strained knee if you hear a popping or snapping sound, feel pain from inside the knee, and are unable to put weight on that leg—or if you feel that your knee is loose. The R.I.C.E. treatment will help, and players with severe injuries may have to use a splint or crutches for a while.

Cartilage injuries to the knee happen when a small piece of cartilage breaks off from the end of the bone. You will be unable to extend the leg. Other symptoms are pain, swelling, stiffness, and a catching sensation when you move. A physician will insist that you rest the knee and wear a cast for about two months. Sometimes surgery is necessary.

Ankle sprains are very common among baseball and softball players. Most twisted ankles are minor sprains, but a team trainer or physician should tape serious sprains. If the ankle is rested, a player can return to competition within days, but if the injury is ignored, recovery could take weeks or months. Treatment is the usual R.I.C.E. program, an ankle brace or tape, and perhaps crutches. Inflammation lasts about three days, and exercises to strengthen the ankle can begin when the player can move without pain.

Recovering from Injuries

The period needed to recover from an injury depends upon how serious it is and the age and physical condition of the player. To help you stay fit as you recover, your physician will devise a rehabilitation program, such as swimming or using a stationary cycle. Specialist physical therapy or the use of ultrasound to heat the injured area may also be recommended.

Tell your physician if pain does not go away after treatment, and follow directions on adjusting your level of play or even discontinuing it. Returning to play too soon could risk another injury or make worse the one from which you are recovering. You might need new protective equipment, such as an elbow brace or knee tape. If the injured area begins to hurt during a game, stop playing immediately. Remember, the best way to return to the diamond is to communicate and cooperate with your coach, parents, and doctor. Ignoring the pain of an injury is one of the worst things you can do.

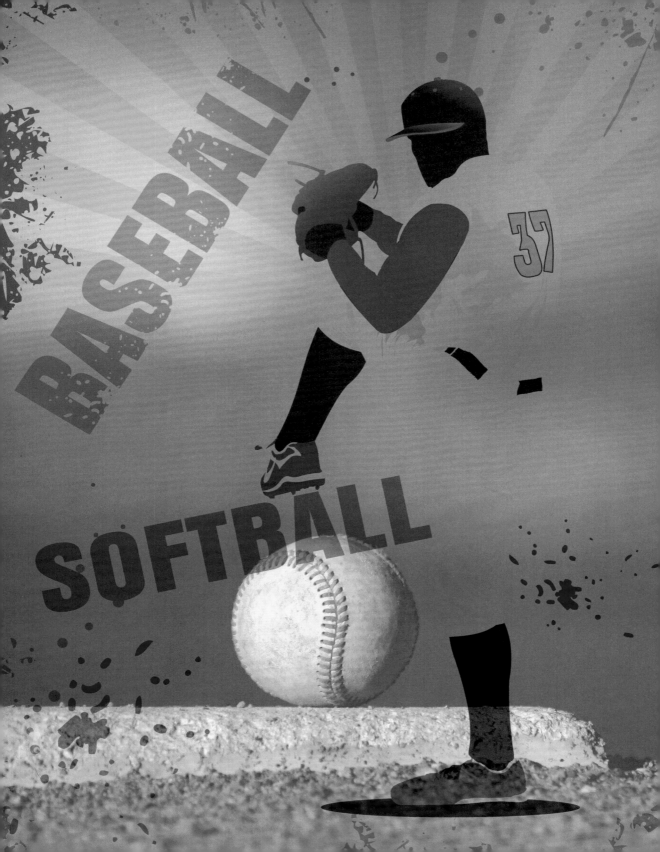

5
Nutrition and Supplements

Understanding the Words

A **nutritionist** *is someone who specializes in helping people eat healthy diets.*

Moderation *means in the middle—not too much, not too little.*

Synthesis *means the process of putting something together.*

Something that is **fortified** *is made stronger than it would have been otherwise.*

Although practice and training are an important part of being safe and successful in the game of baseball, you also need to think about what you take into your body. Athletes must be careful to eat a proper blend of nutrients to make sure their bodies and minds perform as well as they possibly can. This doesn't just mean eating healthy foods but also choosing when to eat, how much to eat, and whether to take dietary supplements. Of course, when you choose a new diet or supplements, you should consult with a **nutritionist**, doctor, or some other expert. Don't make up your own nutrition program!

What to Eat

While a balanced diet is important for everyone, it is even more important for athletes. Typically, an athlete has to eat considerably more than other people do. The United States Food and Drug Administration (FDA) suggests that the average American should eat about 2000 calories a day; for a male high school- or college-level baseball player, a 3000–4000 calorie diet is more common. There are three main food groups to consider when choosing a diet: carbohydrates, protein, and fats.

CARBOHYDRATES

Carbohydrates are foods rich in a chemical called starch, which is what the body breaks down to get energy. Starchy foods include breads and grains, vegetables such as potatoes, cereal, pasta, and rice. Roughly half an athlete's calories should come from carbohydrates, but you should beware of heavily processed carbohydrates such as sugary foods and white bread made with bleached flour. These foods are quickly broken down into sugars, which the body processes into fats if it does not immediately burn them off. The best carbohydrate choices for an athlete are pasta and whole-grain foods, as well as starchy vegetables, which have vitamins as well as carbohydrates. A balanced diet avoids the "empty calories" supplied by white bread and sugars.

Certain types of pastas (specifically whole-grain pastas) are a good source of complex carbohydrates. Half of all the nutrients an athlete takes in should be carbohydrates.

PROTEIN

Proteins are important chemicals found in all living things; these chemicals are used to perform specific functions inside our body cells. Each protein is a long, folded, chain-like molecule made up of "links" called amino acids. Our bodies can break down proteins that are found in foods into their base amino acids and use them to build new proteins that make up our muscles and bones. For this reason, during any exercise regimen, it is important to eat enough protein to give the body the building blocks it needs to become

Milk, cheese, eggs, and meat are all excellent sources of protein. Non-animal products, such as beans, soy, and rice, also contain protein.

stronger. The best sources of proteins are meats and dairy products (such as milk or cheese), as well as eggs and certain vegetables (such as soy, beans, and rice). A good rule of thumb for how much protein to eat is that the number of grams should be equal to about three-quarters of your body weight in pounds. For example, a 200-pound person should eat at least 150 grams of protein every day, or a 120-pound person should have roughly 90 grams of protein.

FATS

Lots of times, we think of fats as bad for us, since eating too much of them is unhealthy. However, fat is an important ingredient needed to make our bod-

Cholesterol

A lot of bad things have been said about cholesterol—but most of this bad press is focused on LDLs, or low-density lipoproteins, which are a kind of cholesterol that can clog our blood vessels and make our hearts work harder. Our bodies make this cholesterol out of saturated fats, such as those found in animal fat from meats, butter, and whole milk. However, there is a kind of cholesterol known as HDLs, or high-density lipoproteins, which have a good effect on the body. Increasing your HDL levels can be as easy as exercising regularly.

ies work correctly. Without fats, our bodies cannot absorb certain vitamins as well. Also, our skin and hair need some amount of fat to grow correctly. However, fats should still be eaten in **moderation**—no more than 70 grams a day. The best sources of fat are vegetable oils, olive oil, and nuts. Many foods contain saturated fats, which lead to the formation of cholesterol and can force your heart to work harder.

Many different kinds of nuts contain protein.

Staying Hydrated

The best diet in the world is no good if you become dehydrated. Dehydration occurs when your body doesn't have enough water, leading to fatigue, dizziness, and headaches, all of which can hurt your performance when playing. It's best to carry a bottle of water with you for the whole day before a practice or game to make sure that you are fully hydrated. In addition, you should be drinking water throughout the game to avoid becoming dehydrated as you sweat. Staying fully hydrated has many benefits besides helping your performance in the game—it can help mental concentration, improves digestive health, and reduces the risk of kidney stones.

Dietary Supplements

Many baseball or softball players seek to improve their performance by taking dietary supplements, which are pills or drinks that contain nutrients or chemicals to improve their physical health or performance in the game. Dietary supplements do not include illegal performance-enhancing drugs. Instead, they contain vitamins and minerals, or chemicals that help the body use vitamins more efficiently. Although when properly used, supplements can improve overall health and performance, you should always consult a doctor or some other expert before taking them. Some examples of common supplements include vitamin tablets, creatine, and protein shakes/powder.

VITAMIN TABLETS

For many reasons, we do not always get the vitamins and nutrients we need. Often, this is because our diets are not as balanced as they should be. Sometimes, it is because the foods that are available to us have been processed in such a way that they lose nutrients. Also, exhausted soil all over the country means that fruits and vegetables are often not as nutrient-rich as they should be. In many cases, we can get the vitamins we need from vitamin supplements. These supplements, which are usually taken as a pill, sometimes contain a balanced mixture of vitamins and nutrients (known as a multivitamin), and sometimes they contain a single vitamin or mineral that our diet is lacking. It is possible to overdose on certain vitamins, however, so be careful when taking vitamin supplements. Don't assume that because a

Vitamin supplements offer an alternative way to get the vitamins that the body needs, but not all dietary supplements are good for you in large amounts. Make sure to speak with a doctor before taking any supplements.

little of something is good for you that a lot of it will be better! Vitamins and minerals don't work that way. And always talk to your doctor before beginning to take supplements of any kind.

CREATINE

Creatine is a specific protein that is naturally found in your body's muscle cells. When taken in larger doses than is found in the body, creatine has the effect of increasing the rate of protein synthesis within your body cells. What this means is that you will have more energy to exercise, and you will see a greater improvement in strength and speed when you do exercise. However, putting any chemical into your body can have negative effects as well, and you should talk to a doctor before beginning to take creatine. What's more, creatine is only suited for adult athletes, so young people (those under the age of 17) should not take it.

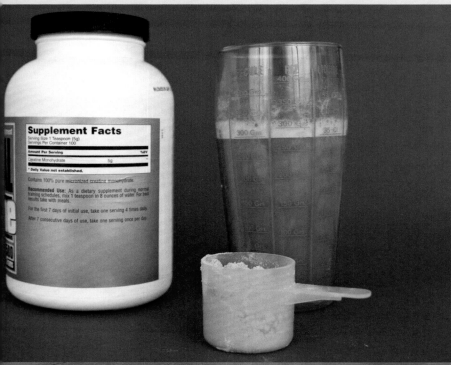

Some dietary supplements (such as protein supplements) come in the form of a drink mix that is combined with water.

Play ball!

Baseball and Alcohol

After a big victory, players may be tempted to celebrate with alcohol. They may also be tempted to use alcohol to ease the pain of defeat. But alcohol intake can interfere with the body's recovery process, and this may interfere with your next game's performance.

It's especially important to avoid any alcohol 24 hours after exercise if you have any soft tissue injuries or bruises. Alcohol and injuries are a bad combination—alcohol may actually increase swelling and bleeding, and it can delay healing.

PROTEIN SUPPLEMENTS

Getting enough protein from the food you eat can be difficult. Eating protein immediately after a workout is recommended (in order to refuel your body), but most people don't feel up to cooking or preparing themselves a meal immediately after a workout. That's why protein shakes are often a convenient choice. Many shakes contain blends of protein, carbohydrates, and fats, and some include vitamins, to help balance an athlete's diet. Furthermore, having protein immediately after a workout can help repair the damage sustained by your muscles during the workout. However, you should remember that while protein shakes are useful for supplementing your diet, they should not be used to replace normal food in any significant quantities. You can get plenty of nutrients from a balanced diet that cannot be replaced by artificial protein shakes, regardless of how **fortified** they may be. A nutritionist can tell you how to fit protein or supplement shakes into your diet safely and effectively.

Play ball!

6
The Dangers of Performance-Enhancing Drugs

Understanding the Words

*Something that is **debilitating** makes you weaker or damages your health.*

*To **stimulate** means to encourage something to happen.*

For many professional players, the pressure to perform well is intense. Athletes face stress from everyone around them to constantly improve their skill, strength, and speed in the game of baseball. From the fans who want their favorite players to win and score good stats, to the coaches and team managers who push their players to perform to their maximum potential, to the players themselves, who are surrounded by other world-class athletes and feel the need to overcome them, the pressure to excel is extreme. Often, an athlete turns to chemical enhancements to reach a level of competitive play that he would not normally be capable of. This is never legal, and is almost always dangerous, but nevertheless, many major-league players feel compelled to participate in performance-enhancing drug use.

What Are Drugs?

In general, a drug is anything that you place into your body that changes your body's chemistry in some way. Drugs can be useful or beneficial, such as the tablets you might take when you have a headache or antibiotics developed to fight diseases. Steroids are drugs useful for certain people with **debilitating** conditions that cause their muscles to waste away, and steroids can also be used to decrease inflammation. However, many drugs, including anabolic steroids, can have serious negative effects on your health.

Steroids

The most common performance enhancers are anabolic steroids. These chemicals are similar to testosterone, which is the male hormone naturally produced by the body to help **stimulate** muscle growth. That's why when a player takes anabolic steroids, he receives a boost to his speed and strength that is greater than what the body could normally produce on its own. Major League Baseball (MLB), as well as almost every other organized sport, considers this cheating.

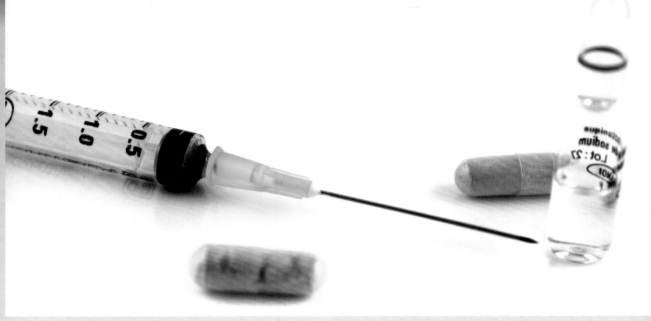

Sometimes called "performance enhancers," many drugs that push the limits of players' abilities (including anabolic steroids) are considered cheating by the MLB.

Steroids can cause an unhealthy increase in cholesterol levels and an increase in blood pressure. This stresses the heart, and leads to an increased risk of heart disease. Large doses of steroids can also lead to liver failure, and they have a negative effect on blood sugar levels, sometimes causing problems similar to diabetes.

If an adolescent (typically someone under the age of about 17) takes anabolic steroids, the risks are often much worse. Steroids stop bones from growing, which results in stunted growth. In addition, the risks to the liver and heart are much greater, since a young person's liver and heart are not fully matured and are more susceptible to the damage that steroids can cause. Furthermore, taking steroids puts you at a greater risk of psychological problems that generally begin with aggression but often lead to much more

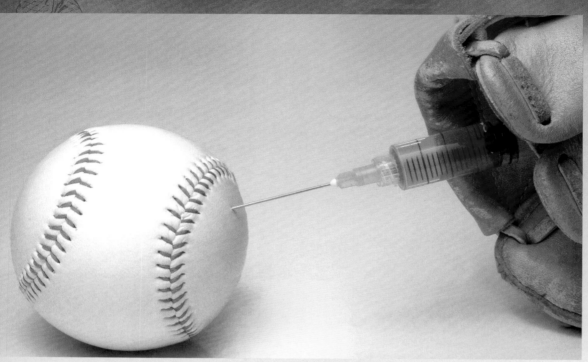

Use of steroids to enhance performance has been banned by almost every major sporting organization in the world, including Major League Baseball.

serious issues. Considering these health risks, as well as the fact that anabolic steroids are almost universally banned from organized sports, they should not be used, except by those who have legitimate medical conditions that require their use.

Human Growth Hormone

Another drug used by some major league players is human growth hormone, or HGH. This chemical is released naturally in the brain when a person is young to tell the rest of the body to grow. However, if an adult takes HGH, it can artificially increase his rate of muscle growth. If someone who has not finished growing takes HGH artificially, it will replace the HGH that is naturally

A-Rod and Drugs

When superstar shortstop Alex Rodriguez—also known as A-Rod—signed a ten-year, $252 million contract with the Texas Rangers in 2000, he became the highest-salaried player in professional sports history. Rodriguez played his first major league baseball game when he was only eighteen, and he became the starting shortstop for the Seattle Mariners when he was twenty. His strength, skill, personality, and Hispanic heritage made fans love him, and Texas owner Tom Hicks signed Rodriguez to an amazing $252 million deal. Rodriguez played well for the Rangers (winning the American League MVP award in 2003), but the team finished last in its division for three straight years, and some blamed Rodriguez's mammoth contract as the reason they couldn't get better players. In 2004, Rodriguez was traded to the New York Yankees, where he moved to third base to play alongside Yankee shortstop Derek Jeter. The deal paid off in 2009, when Rodriguez had a breakthrough postseason, batting .365 (19-for-52) with six home runs and 18 RBIs, and the Yankees won the World Series.

Then the bomb dropped. In January 2009, A-Rod was accused of using banned substances in Texas. He admitted his past drug use and he blamed himself, saying again and again that he had been "young and stupid." Unfortunately, not everyone has been able to forgive Alex—and his stupid mistakes will haunt Alex, who's always been concerned about his reputation, for the rest of his life.

Drugs and Major League Baseball

The MLB's penalties for positive steroid testing in place before 2005 included the following:

- A suspension of ten games the first time a player tests positive for steroids.
- A suspension of thirty games the second time a player tests positive.
- If the player tests positive for steroids a third time, he is suspended for sixty games.
- After a fourth offense, the player would be suspended for one full year.
- The fifth time a player tests positively for steroids, he is given a punishment at the commissioner's discretion.

After the BALCO scandal in 2005, the MLB put in place a much stricter policy. The punishments for testing positively are now:

- The first time a player tests positive for steroid use, he is suspended for fifty games.
- The second time a player tests positive, he is suspended for one hundred games.
- If a players tests positive for steroid use a third time, he receives a lifetime ban from playing baseball.

Play ball!

When a player is suspended, he is prevented from participating in the game, and he does not receive pay for the duration of his suspension. In addition, any other player can replace a suspended player on the team's active roster. These new policies bring the MLB closer to international standards for drug use, as well as the penalties set in place by other major league sports, including the National Football League.

produced by the brain—and when he stops taking it, his brain does not begin producing it again, stunting his growth. People who take HGH also have increased risk of psychological issues.

Illicit Drugs

Sometimes, professional players use other drugs unrelated to boosting performance. The MLB has set severe penalties for using these drugs, and the drugs' side effects will usually decrease performance on the field. That's why professional baseball players don't usually use illegal drugs such as cocaine, LSD, and opiates.

A History of Performance Enhancers

For most of the history of Major League Baseball, steroid testing has never been a major issue. This all changed in early 2005, when the nutrition center BALCO was accused of supplying steroids to quite a few notable baseball players, including Barry Bonds of the San Francisco Giants. Almost immediately after the accusations, Major League Baseball responded by toughening its steroid-testing requirements, and within ten days, a policy of random drug testing was instated. As a result, several players were suspended.

Many critics felt these measures weren't enough, however, and a congressional hearing was convened to hear testimonies from several major baseball players, including Mark McGwire, Sammy Sosa, and Alex Rodriguez. Many of these players admitted to steroid use at some point in their careers,

After Barry Bonds and many other famous professional baseball players were accused of using steroids to gain an advantage over others, the MLB began randomly screening players for steroid use.

while others, including McGwire, refused to speak on the matter. In the end, BALCO was shut down, and the head of the company, Victor Conte, spent four months in prison.

Many of the players accused of anabolic steroid use were never convicted. For example, Barry Bonds, baseball's current record holder for the most career home runs (762), was on the list of BALCO customers who has purchased steroids. However, he never tested positive for steroids, and no one involved in the BALCO scandal bore witness to actually selling Bonds the drugs, so despite the controversy, he was not punished.

Today, while requirements are much stricter than they used to be, it is still impossible to catch every player using steroids. David Wells, a former pitcher for the New York Yankees and Toronto Blue Jays, estimated that between 25 and 40 percent of all major league players were using steroids. In addition, former outfielder José Canseco stated in his book *Juiced* that roughly 85 percent of players had used steroids at some point during their career. Despite these discouraging numbers, with the random testing and stricter penalties in place today, hopefully, drug use in professional sports will decrease significantly.

The American philosopher Ralph Waldo Emerson once said, "Make the most of yourself, for that is all there is of you." This is true when it comes to playing baseball—you are the only raw material with which you can work to become a successful player. Make the most of this raw material by having a positive attitude, practicing, using the right equipment, avoiding injuries, eating healthy, and refusing to take drugs that can ultimately damage your body. Make the most of yourself—and who knows where you may end up!

Further Reading

Coleman, A. Eugene. *52-Week Baseball Training*. Champaign, Ill.: Human Kinetics, 2004.

Goldstein, Warren. *Playing for Keeps: A History of Early Baseball.* Ithaca, N.Y.: Cornell University Press, 2008.

Lewine, Harris. *The Ultimate Baseball Book.* New York: Mariner, 2000.

Price, Rob. *Ultimate Guide to Weight Training for Baseball.* Chicago: Sportsworkout, 2006.

Okrent, Daniel. *Nine Innings.* New York: Mariner, 2000.

Rader, Benjamin G. *Baseball: A History of America's Game.* University of Illinois Press, 2008.

Tamborra, Steve. *Complete Conditioning for Baseball.* Champaign, Ill.: Human Kinetics, 2007.

Tango, Tom M. *The Book: Playing the Percentages in Baseball.* Potomac Books, 2007.

Vecsey, George. *Baseball: A History of America's Game.* New York: Modern Library, 2008.

Play ball!

Find Out More on the Internet

Baseball Almanac
www.baseball-almanac.com/

Baseball Encyclopedia of MLB Players
baseball-reference.com/players.shtml

Baseball Injuries
www.faqs.org/sports-science/A-Ba.../Baseball-Injuries.html

Baseball Injury Prevention
orthoinfo.aaos.org/topic.cfm?topic=A00185

Baseball Training & Conditioning
www.sport-fitness-advisor.com/baseball-training.html

Baseball Training Secrets
www.baseballtrainingsecrets.com/

Common Baseball Injuries
sportsmedicine.about.com/od/baseballinjuries/a/baseballinjury.htm

The History of Baseball
www.rpi.edu/~fiscap/history_files/history1.htm

How Performance-Enhancing Drugs Work
www.howstuffworks.com › Entertainment › Sports › Olympics

The Official Site of Major League Baseball
www.mlb.com/

What Are Performance-Enhancing Drugs?
www.wisegeek.com/what-are-performance-enhancing-drugs.htm

Who Invented Baseball?
inventors.about.com/library/inventors/blbaseball.htm

Disclaimer
The websites listed on this page were active at the time of publication. The publisher is not responsible for websites that have changed their address or discontinued operation since the date of publication. The publisher will review and update the websites upon each reprint.

Play ball!

Bibliography

Baseball Almanac, "History." www.baseball-almanac.com (15 January 2010).

The Baseball Archive, "General History." www.baseball1.com/c-history.html (16 January 2010).

Family Education, "Common Baseball Injuries." life.familyeducation.com/wounds-and-injuries/first-aid/48319.html (17 January 2010).

"The History of Baseball." www.rpi.edu/~fiscap/history_files/history1.htm (15 January 2010).

Mitchell Report, "Performance-Enhancing Drugs in the Major Leagues." mlb.mlb.com/mlb/news/mitchell/coverage.jsp (18 January 2010).

Orthopedic Connection, "Baseball Injury Prevention." orthoinfo.aaos.org/topic.cfm?topic=A00185 (18 January 2010).

Sports Fitness Advisor, "Baseball Training & Conditioning." www.sport-fitness-advisor.com/baseball-training.html (16 January 2010)

Sports Medicine, "Baseball Injuries." sportsmedicine.about.com/baseballinjuries/Baseball_Injuries.htm (17 January 2010).

The Steroid Era, "Baseball." thesteroidera.blogspot.com (18 January 2010).

Training Secrets, "Baseball Training." www.baseballtrainingsecrets.com (16 January 2010).

Play ball!

Index

Picture Credits

CCYBSA:
  Keith Allison: pg. 29
  Kevin Rushforth: pg. 88

Dreamstime:
  Celsopupo: pg. 74
  Hivoltage: pg. 78

Fotolia:
  Actionpic: pp. 23 and 30
  Andrew Brown: pg. 83
  Brenda Carson pg. 27
  Claus Aagaard: pg. 16
  James Steidl: pg. 67
  Jason Stitt: pg. 38
  John Young: pg. 18
  Konstantin Kukushkin: pg. 75
  Kzenon: pg. 54
  London_England: pg. 62
  Maridav: pg. 53
  Mark Lanning: pg. 41
  Michael Chamberlin: pg. 48
  Michael Flippo: pg. 13

Paylessimages: pg. 49
Peter Kim: pg. 43
peter lecko: pg. 61
Phantom: pg. 39
Ramon Grosso: pg. 60
Rebecca Hanson: pg. 50
Rob Byron: pg. 84
Silvia Bogdanski: pg. 73
Sly: pp. 34 and 38
Steve Cukrov: pg. 40
TravellingLens: pg. 65
VICKY ANDRIOTIS: pg. 77
zmu: pg. 19

To the best knowledge of the publisher, all images not specifically credited are in the public domain. If any image has been inadvertently uncredited, please notify Harding House Publishing Service, 220 Front Street, Vestal, New York 13850, so that credit can be given in future printings.

Play ball!

About the Author and the Consultants

Gabriel Sanna is an independent author living in upstate New York. Professionally, he is torn between his love of computers and his love of writing, but so far he is managing to combine both interests. In high school, he was on the cross-country team, and he still runs regularly, preferring woodland trails to tracks. Besides sports, he has written on a variety of topics.

Susan Saliba, Ph.D., is a senior associate athletic trainer and a clinical instructor at the University of Virginia in Charlottesville, Virginia. A certified athletic trainer and licensed physical therapist, Dr. Saliba provides sports medicine care, including prevention, treatment, and rehabilitation for the varsity athletes at the university. Dr. Saliba is a member of the national Athletic Trainers' Association Educational Executive Committee and its Clinical Education Committee.

Eric Small, M.D., a Harvard-trained sports medicine physician, is a nationally recognized expert in the field of sports injuries, nutritional supplements, and weight management programs. He is author of *Kids & Sports* (2002) and is Assistant Clinical professor of pediatrics, Orthopedics, and Rehabilitation Medicine at Mount Sinai School of Medicine in New York. He is also Director of the Sports Medicine Center for Young Athletes at Blythedale Children's Hospital in Valhalla, New York. Dr. Small has served on the American Academy of Pediatrics Committee on Sports Medicine, where he develops national policy regarding children's medical issues and sports.